THE ABUNDANT LIFE

leader guide

"I have come that they may have life, and that they may have it more abundantly."

John 10:10

Greg E. Viehman, M.D.

Author:	Greg E. Viehman, M.D.
Editor:	Greg McElveen
Reviewers:	Kathy Phipps and Sarah Land
Cover Illustration, design © 2015	Marketing Ministries
Cover Photo © 2015	Shutterstock.com
Interior photos © 2015	Shutterstock.com

Library of Congress Control Numbers:

1. BS2525-2544 Study and teaching
2. BT750-811 Salvation. Soteriology
3. BT1095-1255 Apologetics. Evidences of Christianity
4. BV205-287 Prayer
5. BV4625-4627 Sins and vices

BISAC / Classification Suggestions:

1. REL006700 RELIGION / Biblical Studies / Bible Study Guides
2. REL012000 RELIGION / Christian Life / General
3. REL012070 RELIGION / Christian Life / Personal Growth
4. REL012120 RELIGION / Christian Life / Spiritual Growth
5. REL099000 RELIGION / Christian Life / Spiritual Warfare

ISBN-13: 978-1-937355-27-2 V 1.0

Big Mac Publishers Book Titles may be purchased in bulk at great discounts by retail vendors, or for educational, business, fund-raising, spiritual or sales promotions. Contact info @ Big Mac Publisher's website. www.bigmacpublishers.com.

INTRODUCTION

Welcome to The Abundant Life! I am so excited for you to be a leader of this Bible study. Your role will be very important to the growth of your group. The goal is to produce "on fire" and healthy disciples of Jesus Christ that are living for the Lord and His glory. This is an amazingly fun, exciting, challenging, and often difficult life. As a leader, setting the right tone is crucial. If you are excited, joyful and energetic, that will be contagious to your group. They will want what you have, will realize it is divinely inspired, and then seek the Lord even more diligently.

This Leader's Guide was written to assist leaders in effectively working with Christians to inspire them to understand how to live an abundant life in Christ. Everything in here, however, is just a guide. Please feel free to use the study and conduct it as the Lord leads you to. Start praying about how to lead your group now! I believe that the more you pray and ask for God's help with your group, the more God will bless you both. This guide covers your first meeting, which will be an introduction and orientation session, and then reviews each week's lessons from a leader's point of view. Let's get started studying and living The Abundant Life!

Greg E. Viehman, M.D.

TABLE OF CONTENTS

GENERAL COMMENTS

Everyone involved at this level should have a copy of the leader's guide. It is vital that you watch the group leader's video in the leader's section of the website. This can be found under "resources" at abundantlifestudy.com. Be excited and amazed at the grace and love of God. Live The Abundant Life before your group each week. Enthusiasm and diligent preparation are so important.

There is a lot of information in the study. We could spend the rest of our lives teaching and exploring the depths of God's Word on these topics. The Abundant Life is designed to be an overview that gets people excited and started on a lifelong journey to know God. During the small group sessions you won't be able to review everything or cover all of the questions. This happens often in Bible study groups and is completely normal so please relax if you don't get in "all the things" you planned or wanted to. An exact time frame for each week's meeting is not suggested since every group is different, but somewhere around 90 minutes should be sufficient for most groups. Your diligent preparation will help with time management, and the best leaders never forget to let the Holy Spirit guide the group. A good leader will balance time constraints without interrupting a group's dynamic interactions.

The Abundant Life is also not designed to be a "show up and learn study." We want people working for short periods of time all week long by digging into their Bible with the Lord as their guide and teacher. The group sessions are meant to solidify and reinforce what they are learning on their own and provide a time for group interaction and edification. Encourage your group to be prepared. Emphasize they will get out of it what they put into it.

LEADERS

You will need a single leader for the entire study. This will be the point person who organizes, supervises, and facilitates the study as a whole. The study leader will also need to appoint small group facilitators when the group is large enough to split into small groups. Very commonly the study leader will also be a small group facilitator. The group facilitators should work together with the study leader to make sure the study runs smoothly and that everyone understands their role and how to participate. Although this leader's guide is written to facilitate larger groups, it can be used in smaller groups as well.

You may have a team leading the study depending upon the size of your group. I encourage you to work and pray as a team for the entire group and for the Lord's blessing on the study. It is suggested that the study leader and group facilitators arrive before the study starts to get everything setup, discuss questions about the week's lessons, and pray. Then be ready to greet everyone warmly with an energetic attitude.

Consider getting everyone's contact information and sending them an encouraging email or text during the week. This is best captured during initial registration. This can be very uplifting and motivating to your group. The small group facilitators are the best people to be the weekly communicators with those in their group.

LAYOUT AND STRUCTURE OF THE STUDY

The study has 27 lessons divided into three parts over ten weeks (11 weeks if you include a separate session for an introduction and orientation). Part I is Abundant Revelation: The Grace of God, Part II Abundant Response: A Relationship with God, and Part III Abundant Results: The Transformation from God. The basic premise is that if someone learns first about how much God has done for them and how awesome He is, then they will respond to God in a relationship from love, gratitude, and eagerness instead of obligation and expectation. This response and relationship creates a state of "spiritual health" that allows them to grow, mature, and be transformed by God. Read the introduction section of the study guide and watch the introduction and group leader video for more information.

Pages 10-11 of this guide have the layout and structure of the study. These are also found in the study manual itself and are available as pdf's under resources at abundantlifestudy.com. Feel free to conduct The Abundant Life study in any time frame that you desire. The format is only a suggestion and guide.

See videos & more under resources at abundantlifestudy.com

Individual Study. Each participant needs a copy of The Abundant Life Study guide. The study guide contains all of the lessons, reading, and questions that will be completed at home during the week in preparation for the group session. Each week has two-to-five lessons that should take 30-45 minutes each to complete.

Group Sessions. Everyone meets together once a week to review, discuss, and apply what they have learned during the week. Group members share actual moments or situations during the past week that validate what they have studied. This meeting will begin each week with the entire group together and then split into small groups. Small groups allow a more intimate setting that promotes relationships and better discussions and sharing.

GROUP SIZES

You should start the study each week as an entire group. There is something about being together that builds excitement and anticipation for what God wants to say to the group as a whole as well as to the individual members. After starting the study as an entire group, a small group discussion time will follow.

Depending upon the size of your entire group you may need to split up into smaller groups for the discussion time. The ideal size to review questions and discuss personal insights is 8 people. Keep in mind not everyone comes every week. You don't want your groups so small that if 1-2 people don't show up there are only 2-3 people in a group. On the other hand, if your groups are too large they can lose their effectiveness because there's not enough time for everyone to contribute.

You will also need to appoint a small group facilitator for each small group to lead the discussions. Usually the leader of the study also serves as one of the small group leaders. Have all of this figured out before your first session so that you can get people acquainted with their small groups on the first orientation night. This is why it's important to have people sign up before the study begins.

FIRST GROUP MEETING: INTRODUCTION AND ORIENTATION

Your first meeting will be an introduction and group orientation to The Abundant Life study. There is enough material to cover to warrant a separate session before the actual lessons begin. This will ensure that your group gets off to a strong start and everyone understands how the study works and what to expect. This orientation session is covered in detail next.

RESOURCES FOR PROMOTING THE STUDY

The Abundant Life website has different resources to help you promote the study. Power Point-ready advertisements, posters, flyers, logos and artwork can be downloaded at abundantlifestudy.com under the resources tab. These will make it easy to advertise the study in church bulletins, projection screens, flyers, posters, email, and social media venues. If you start early you will build up excitement!

RESOURCES FOR TEACHING THE STUDY

There are also several resources to help you teach the study. All of the charts, diagrams, and outlines are available as pdf's under resources at abundantlifestudy. com. There is also a PowerPoint template and presentation for the first meeting that serves as an introduction and group orientation. This session is discussed next.

See videos & more under resources at abundantlifestudy.com

OUTLINE

Part I. Abundant Revelation
Abundant Grace:

WEEK 1
- Abundant Need
- Abundant Provision
- **Salvation Evaluation**

WEEK 2
- Abundant Change
- Abundant Newness
- Abundant Worth

WEEK 3
- Abundant Wealth
- Abundant Power
- Abundant Freedom

WEEK 4
- Abundant Security
- Abundant Hope
- Abundant Plans

Part II. Abundant Response (God & Man)
Abundant Relationship:

WEEK 5
- Abundant Surrender
- Abundant Praise
- Abundant Words

WEEK 6
- Abundant God
- Abundant Repentance
- Abundant Love for God
- Abundant Health
- **Heart Examination**

Part III. Abundant Results
Abundant Transformation:

WEEK 7
- Abundant Growth
- Abundant Godliness

WEEK 8
- Abundant Struggle
- Abundant Suffering
- Abundant Victory

Abundant Fruit:

WEEK 9
- Abundant Love for Others
- Abundant Giving

WEEK 10
- Abundant Service
- Abundant Harvest

THE ABUNDANT LIFE PATHWAY

PART I
ABUNDANT REVELATION

PART II
ABUNDANT RESPONSE

ABUNDANT HEALTH

PART III
ABUNDANT RESULTS

See videos & more
under resources at
abundantlifestudy.com

THE ABUNDANT LIFE
VIDEO LIST

There are 16 videos for the study available under resources at abundantlifestudy.com.

Video 1	Introduction
Video 2	Part I Overview
Video 3	Week 1
Video 4	Salvation Evaluation
Video 5	Week 2
Video 6	Week 3
Video 7	Week 4
Video 8	Part II Overview
Video 9	Week 5
Video 10	Week 6
Video 11	Heart Examination
Video 12	Part III Overview
Videos 13-15	Weeks 7-10
Video 16	Conclusion

FIRST MEETING

INTRODUCTION & GROUP ORIENTATION

Counting the first session as an introduction and orientation, the study will be 11 weeks long. Please plan and schedule your group for 11 sessions. There is enough to review and discuss to warrant an introductory and orientation session so that your group gets off to a solid start. All of this material is available in a PowerPoint presentation under the resources tab at abundantlifestudy.com. Here is what you should consider covering in this session:

1. **Welcome:** Welcome everyone to the study. Have a quick time of introductions and provide nametags to help people get to know each other if necessary. This should be done as people are arriving.

   Encourage people to keep their cell phones on silent and to put them away during the study. Texting and emailing during the study is highly discouraged. It is recommended that the group instruct their family to only call them if there is an emergency. It is very distracting if everyone is constantly on their phones during the study. It is also essential to start on time. There is a tendency for this to begin to drift later and later as a study progresses. Emphasize that starting at 8 O'Clock, for example, means arriving at 7:50, not 8.

2. **Pass out The Abundant Life study guides to your group.**

3. **Introductory Video:** Watch the introduction video together as an overview of the study. Familiarize yourself with this video and the material in the introduction section of the study guide prior to the meeting. They are similar in content. Provide any further introductory comments as needed to make sure the group understands what the study is trying to achieve and the method behind it. The basic premise is that if we learn what God has done for us and what He is like (Part I) then we will respond in gratitude and love to God. Our response opens the door to a relationship with God and state of spiritual health (Part II). The healthy Christian then begins to grow, produce fruit, and be

See videos & more under resources at abundantlifestudy.com

transformed into the likeness of Jesus by the power of the Holy Spirit (Part III).

Review and explain The Abundant Life Pathway. This is found on page 13 of the study guide. There is also a pdf and PowerPoint slide of the "pathway" on the website under "resources" at abundantlife study.com.

4. **Review Study Structure:** Review the structure of the study that lays out the next 10 weeks. This is found on page 14 of the study guide and is also available in the resources section as a pdf and PowerPoint slide. This will illustrate the big picture of what the study will cover each week.

5. **Review Weekly Individual Study:**

   A. Videos: First explain the way videos will be used in the study. There is one video for each week of the study, and also a separate video for each of the three major parts of the study that provides an overview of the entire section (e.g. Part I, II, and III overview videos). (They will watch Part I Overview later during this introductory session.)

   The videos should be watched before they start studying each week. They were designed to be a primer for each week's study. You should also alert them that there are two special videos for the Salvation Evaluation and Heart Examination section of the study. The study guide also alerts the reader concurrently when there are videos that need to be watched.

   Review the list of the videos and where to find them on the website. This is found on page 11 of the study guide. You also have access to this list as a pdf and PowerPoint slide if needed.

   **It is recommended that you show the videos as a refresher at the start of each week. Although everyone is supposed to watch them at home before the group meeting, this does not always occur. Watching them twice will not be redundant since they are short and useful to view more than once. Most weeks only have one video that averages seven

to ten minutes in length. A few weeks have more than one video that can add up to twenty minutes total time. Plan your time management accordingly these weeks.**

B. **Weekly Lessons Structure:** Explain the structure of each week in the study guide. This study has 27 lessons. Most weeks have between two-to-four lessons. Each lesson follows the same format:

Short Introduction: One to two paragraphs describing the lesson and key points to understand.

Verses To Read, Study, and Meditate On: A series of biblical principles are taught. Each principle has several Bible verses to look up. The Bible verses are the specific Scriptures that pertain to what is being discussed. Emphasize to your group that they should look up all of the verses if possible. There are some verses that are in parentheses that are optional since they are redundant. The study guide also explains this in the introduction. You want to encourage the group to dig into the Word of God.

Please also instruct your group to never just read the verses listed in isolation. For each of the verses, please have them read the entire paragraph in which they are found to get the context of what is being taught. They may need to read the entire chapter. The verses are listed to pinpoint the key idea in that part of the Scriptures. Have them read each of them several times and meditate on them. If a verse is listed several times in a lesson, instruct them to read it every time it is listed. Many verses teach more than one point at a time, and it is always useful to review.

Questions to Ponder: The next section at the end of each week consists of a series of questions. There is space to record their answers. These questions are important and will be discussed the following week in the small group sessions.

C. **Reflections:** This section comes at the end of each weekly lesson. It is a place for the participants to record insights and applications from the week's lessons. This is designed to serve as a journal or

See videos & more under resources at abundantlifestudy.com

record of what the Lord has shown your group during the week and how they can apply it practically to their lives. This is very important. Please encourage your group to take the time to do this at the end of each week. Their answers will also be used in the small group discussions.

The Abundant Life study is designed to be a home study with a weekly review and interaction in a group setting. The majority of the learning is intended to be one on one at home between the Lord and the student. It is not intended to be a "show up and learn on the fly" study. It is critical to encourage your group to do everything in the study. If they just show up, they will not get nearly as much out of it.

6. **Review Weekly Group Sessions:**
Now that you have reviewed what they will be doing at home, go over what will happen each week when you come together to meet. That way they will know what to expect and where to go, etc.

A. General Group Meeting: Explain that everyone will meet in one place to start off each week. The meeting will start off with prayer and then the videos for that week will be shown as a review and preview. Leaders might also provide some general comments at this point.

B. Small Group Sessions: Each week your group will split up into their assigned small groups. Explain that groups of approximately eight will meet together to review each lesson and answer the questions. The format for this will be as follows:

Emphasize
Key Points: The group leader will briefly review the key points for the lesson.

Key Verses: The group will take turns reading four-to-six key verses aloud from the lesson.

Engage

Key Questions: The group leader will ask a few key questions to stimulate discussion. Some of the questions at the end of each lesson will be reviewed.

Key Insights: The group will share their insights from the lesson.

Key Applications: The group will share how they will apply what they have learned.

This format is repeated for each of the weekly lessons. Twenty-to-thirty minutes per lesson is about the right amount of time to spend, but keep it flexible. Each small group can pray and adjourn on their own. This avoids groups that finish early having to wait for those groups that are taking longer. The next page provides a summary of how the study functions each week.

At this point, give everyone their small group assignments. Review the small groups and where they will be meeting. Introduce the facilitators for each of the small groups. Make sure everybody knows what group they are in, who their facilitator is, and where they will be meeting after the general session adjourns each week.

See videos & more under resources at abundantlifestudy.com

7. **Watch Part I Overview Video:** This will be a preview of what they will cover the first week. Please inform them that Week One is a little different than the regular weeks. It has two lessons and a Salvation Evaluation. Lesson 1 reviews the state of a person before they are saved. Lesson 2 presents the Gospel and what Jesus did to provide salvation. Next, the Salvation Evaluation is designed to teach everyone how to really know if they are truly a genuine born again Christian. Salvation Evaluation has its own video that is 13 minutes long. You should preview this and all the videos for Week 1 before you conduct this introduction and orientation session. The Salvation Evaluation video is highly evangelistic and challenges people to examine themselves. A salvation opportunity is included at the end. This video is designed for a person to watch on their own at home after completing lessons 1 and 2.

8. **Closing Comments:** End with an encouraging word, Scripture, and prayer.

WEEKLY STRUCTURE OF THE ABUNDANT LIFE STUDY
Summary

I. INDIVIDUAL STUDY (AT HOME):

Step 1: Watch Video(s) for the Week online at
abundantlifestudy.com.

Step 2: Work through 2-4 lessons each week. Read,
look up Bible verses, and answer questions.

Step 3: Write down insights and applications in
Reflections section of study guide.

II. GROUP STUDY: 90 MINUTES

A. General Group Meeting: 20-30 minutes

Step 1: Opening prayer and comments

Step 2: Watch video(s) for the week as a group

Step 3: Break out into small groups

B. Small Group Sessions: 60 minutes

Step 1: Review and answer questions from each lesson
(20-30 minutes per lesson)

Step 2: Adjourn

The times are only suggestions. Feel free to be flexible.

See videos & more
under resources at
abundantlifestudy.com

THE
ABUNDANT
LIFE
leader guide

PART 1
WEEKS 1-4

PART I
ABUNDANT REVELATION
Abundant Grace

WEEK 1

Lesson 1 • Abundant Need
The Need for Grace

Lesson 2 • Abundant Provision
The Rescue of Grace

Salvation Evaluation

WEEK 1 OVERVIEW

Prepare: It is critical to have thoroughly prepared yourself to lead this study. Do the study, look up all the verses, watch the videos, and answer the questions. Don't forget you are also a student in the study. Ask the Lord to reveal His Word to you as you study. Become very familiar with the major topics, themes, and verses for this week's lessons. Be in prayer all week for you and your group.

Pray: Open the session in prayer. Consider asking one of the participants to pray for the study.

Preview: Watch the video for week 1 as a preview and review. Note: there are two videos for this week: Week 1 video and the Salvation Evaluation video. The Salvation Evaluation is 13 minutes long. Use it at your discretion considering time constraints. Both videos combined are twenty minutes long.

After watching the videos together, split into small groups if applicable. The small group leaders should guide the discussion and provide time management to stay on course. Remember you can't cover everything. The goal is to have good discussion and participation in each of the lessons.

Lesson 1 • Abundant Need
The Need for Grace

Key Points: The depravity of the human condition before salvation is the key emphasis. You want people to realize how fallen we are from what we were created to be. We are born spiritually dead (separated from God), eternally condemned, and physically dying in a fallen human body that has a sinful nature and a sin debt that we can never repay. Part of our depravity is that we think our current life here on earth is "normal." We have been surrounded by fallen people just like us since we were born. We may realize that we have bad behavior but seldom realize the depth and extent of our sin and separation from God. We are fallen at the level of our person and at the very core of our existence. The more your group understands this and assimilates it into their hearts and paradigms of life, the more grateful they will be to Jesus Christ for salvation. Whoever is forgiven much, loves much and whoever is forgiven little, loves little. Read and study Luke 7:36-50 in preparation. The truth is that any person that has received the salvation of God through Jesus Christ has been forgiven more than they can ever comprehend. This means we should have unlimited love for God.

Key Verses: Have your group take turns reading the following verses aloud to the group: Ephesians 2:1-3; Psalm 51:5; Isaiah 59:2; Romans 3:9-20; John 3:16-19.

ENGAGE

Key Questions: *Why is it so important to see the depth of our depravity?* Also review answers to the questions at the end of the lesson. You will likely need to focus your time on one or two of them that are the most interesting to your group.

Key Insights: Ask the group to share what struck them the most about our Abundant Need.

Key Applications: Ask the group to share how they plan to apply what they have learned. They should have prepared for this in the Reflections section of the study, which is at the end of each week's lessons.

See videos & more under resources at abundantlifestudy.com

Lesson 2 • Abundant Provision
The Rescue of Grace

Key Points: The incredible cost of salvation is the emphasis of this week's lesson. The price paid reveals the magnitude of the debt (Lesson 1) from another perspective. This lesson should magnify the group's understanding of our abundant need and begin to reveal the love and grace of God, who met that need in Jesus Christ on the cross.

Key Verses: Have your group take turns reading the following verses aloud to the group: Isaiah 53:3-12; Ephesians 2:4-5; John 3:13-17; Romans 5:6-8; Luke 22:41-44; 1 Corinthians 15:3-8.

ENGAGE

Key Question: **What does the cross reveal about human depravity and the love of God?** Also review answers to the questions at the end of the lesson. You will likely need to focus your time on one or two of them that are the most interesting to your group.

Key Insights: Ask the group to share what struck them the most about God's Abundant Provision.

Key Applications: Ask the group to share how they plan to apply what they have learned. They should have prepared for this in the Reflections section of the study, which is at the end of each week's lessons.

Salvation Evaluation

EMPHASIZE

Key Points: There is a great deception about salvation. Many people are living in Churchianity instead of the relationship of Christianity. Jesus warned that people would trust in their Christian deeds and religious activities instead of their relationship and obedience to God by faith. The goal is for everyone to evaluate themselves before God and make sure they truly belong to Him.

Key Verses: Have your group take turns reading the following verses aloud to the group: 2 Corinthians 13:5; Matthew 7:21-23; Ephesians 2:8-9; James 2:19; 2 Corinthians 7:10.

ENGAGE

Key Question: ***How do you know if you are truly born again (i.e "saved")?***
Encourage the group to give short testimonies. Start by giving yours if appropriate.

Key Insights: Ask the group to share what struck them the most about Salvation Evaluation. Does anyone in your group know someone who is lost in Christian religion?

Key Applications: Ask the group to share how they plan to apply what they have learned. They should have prepared for this in the Reflections section of the study, which is at the end of each week's lessons.

See videos & more
under resources at
abundantlifestudy.com

WEEK 2

Lesson 3 • Abundant Change
The Results of Grace

Lesson 4 • Abundant Newness
The Transformation of Grace

Lesson 5 • Abundant Worth
The Worthiness of Grace

WEEK 2 OVERVIEW

Prepare: Your preparation for the study is very important for your group and your own growth. You are studying some of the most amazing facts that a human being can ponder! Dig deep into God's Word and ask Him to reveal the incredible changes and blessings of salvation. Be in prayer all week for you and your group.

Pray: Open the session in prayer. Consider asking one of the participants to pray for the study.

Preview: Watch the video for week 2 as a preview and review. There is only one video this week. It will add ten minutes to the study.

After watching the video together, split into small groups if applicable. The small group leaders should guide the discussion and provide time management to stay on course. Remember you can't cover everything. The goal is to have good discussion and participation in each of the lessons.

Lesson 3 • Abundant Change
The Results of Grace

Key Points: Salvation is much more than the forgiveness of sins. It is a transformation of our existence and relationship with God from separation, enmity, and spiritual death to eternal life that starts at that moment by God living within us. An incredible truth! You want your group to be amazed at these spiritual truths.

Key Verses: Have your group take turns reading the following verses aloud to the group: Psalm 103:12; Romans 3:21-26, 6:23; Ephesians 1:7, 1:13-14.

Key Questions: ***Why is it so important to understand all of the changes from salvation in addition to the forgiveness of sins?*** Also review answers to the questions at the end of the lesson. You will likely need to focus your time on one or two of them that are the most interesting to your group.

Key Insights: Ask the group to share what struck them the most about Abundant Change. What is the most profound change to them?

Key Applications: Ask the group to share how they plan to apply what they have learned. They should have prepared for this in the Reflections section of the study, which is at the end of each week's lessons.

See videos & more
under resources at
abundantlifestudy.com

Lesson 4 • Abundant Newness
The Transformation of Grace

Key Points: Being a Christian is not something you believe but someone you become. God radically changes the nature of our existence when we are saved. The more we understand the incredible grace and provision of God, the more motivated we will be to serve Him and surrender our lives to Him from gratitude, awe, wonder, and love. You want your group to be blown away by these changes.

Key Verses: Have your group take turns reading the following verses aloud to the group: 2 Corinthians 5:17; Romans 5:10-11, 6:4-8; Ezekiel 36:26-27; John 1:12-13.

ENGAGE

Key Question: **What isn't new as a result of salvation?** Also review answers to the questions at the end of the lesson. You will likely need to focus your time on one or two of them that are the most interesting to your group.

Key Insights: Ask the group to share what struck them the most about Abundant Newness.

Key Applications: Ask the group to share how they plan to apply what they have learned. They should have prepared for this in the Reflections section of the study, which is at the end of each week's lessons.

Lesson 5 • Abundant Worth
The Worthiness of Grace

EMPHASIZE

Key Points: God has made us important and valuable people in Christ. God has declared that we are very valuable to Him, and He has revealed that as Christians we have invaluable roles and responsibilities. You want to teach your group to get their sense of worth from the Lord. Our society tries to get this in all the wrong places, and none of them provide a true sense of worth that lasts or is meaningful in the heart.

Key Verses: Have your group take turns reading the following verses aloud to the group: Ephesians 2:10; 2 Corinthians 5:18-21; 1 John 3:1-3; 1 Corinthians 6:19-20; Matthew 5:13-16.

ENGAGE

Key Question: *What's the difference between getting your worth from God and getting it from the world?* Also review answers to the questions at the end of the lesson. You will likely need to focus your time on one or two of them that are the most interesting to your group.

Key Insights: Ask the group to share what struck them the most about Abundant Worth.

Key Applications: Ask the group to share how they plan to apply what they have learned. They should have prepared for this in the Reflections section of the study, which is at the end of each week's lessons.

See videos & more
under resources at
abundantlifestudy.com

WEEK 3

Lesson 6 • Abundant Wealth
The Riches of Grace

Lesson 7 • Abundant Power
The Empowerment of Grace

Lesson 8 • Abundant Freedom
The Liberty of Grace

WEEK 3 OVERVIEW

Prepare: The Abundant Life should be contagious! You want your group to "catch it" from you. If you are excited, your group will be too. The more you prepare and dig into these lessons and Scriptures the more excited and contagious you will be. Be in prayer all week for you and your group.

Pray: Open the session in prayer. Consider asking one of the participants to pray for the study.

Preview: Watch the video for week 3 as a preview and review. There is only one video this week. It will add seven minutes to the study. Everyone should have watched it at home.

After watching the video together, split into small groups if applicable. The small group leaders should guide the discussion and provide time management to stay on course. Remember you can't cover everything. The goal is to have good discussion and participation in each of the lessons.

Lesson 6 • Abundant Wealth
The Riches of Grace

Key Points: Salvation is much more than the forgiveness of sins. It is a transformation of our existence and relationship with God from separation, enmity, and spiritual death to eternal life that starts at that moment by God living within us. An incredible truth! You want your group to be amazed at these spiritual truths.

Key Verses: Have your group take turns reading the following verses aloud to the group: Ephesians 1:15-23; Hebrews 4:16; 1 John 5:11-13; Ephesians 1:13-14; 2 Timothy 3:16-17.

ENGAGE

Key Questions: ***How are we spiritually rich in Jesus Christ? How can we keep these riches vibrant and practical in the Christian life?*** Also review answers to the questions at the end of the lesson. You will likely need to focus your time on one or two of them that are the most interesting to your group.

Key Insights: Ask the group to share what struck them the most about Abundant Wealth. Which of the "riches" is the most profound and amazing to them? Which one is the most practical? Why?

Key Applications: Ask the group to share how they plan to apply what they have learned. They should have prepared for this in the Reflections section of the study, which is at the end of each week's lessons.

See videos & more under resources at abundantlifestudy.com

Lesson 7 • Abundant Power
The Empowerment of Grace

EMPHASIZE

Key Points: God did not just forgive our sins. He gave us abundant power over sin to live the Christian life right now. This power is from the Holy Spirit living within us. It is available but we must tap into it by living The Abundant Life. Many Christians don't know the power that is available. They try to live the Christian life in their own power and end up miserable and defeated. We will study how the power of God is unleashed later in the study. For now make your group aware of all the areas that power is available to them. Get them excited to experience it and be grateful for it. Emphasize that the power comes from the person of God living within them.

Key Verses: Have your group take turns reading the following verses aloud to the group: 2 Peter 1:3-4; 2 Timothy 1:7; Romans 8:12-17; Nehemiah 8:10; Hebrews 4:12.

ENGAGE

Key Question: *Can we fully utilize power that we don't know is available to us?* Also review answers to the questions at the end of the lesson. You will likely need to focus your time on one or two of them that are the most interesting to your group.

Key Insights: Ask the group to share why they think we are often unaware of the power available to us? Which aspect of God's power is the most important and practical to them?

Key Applications: Ask the group to share how they plan to apply what they have learned. They should have prepared for this in the Reflections section of the study, which is at the end of each week's lessons.

Lesson 8 • Abundant Freedom
The Liberty of Grace

Key Points: Freedom comes from abiding in the Word of God and having our minds and hearts renewed as we learn and apply Scripture. The Lord has given us freedom from life's most basic worries, fears, and problems. Everyone struggles with sin, its consequences, and with issues of our self-perception (worth, adequacy, etc). Get your group excited and grateful that God has set us free from all of this baggage and corruption!

Key Verses: Have your group take turns reading the following verses aloud to the group: John 8:31-32; Romans 6:1-14, 8:1-4, 8:28-39; Philippians 4:4-7.

ENGAGE

Key Question: *What does freedom from all of these things mean? How do we get set free? In which areas are you still in bondage when you could be free?* Also review answers to the questions at the end of the lesson. You will likely need to focus your time on one or two of them that are the most interesting to your group.

Key Insights: Ask the group to share which aspect of Abundant Freedom is most profound to them. Which is the most helpful to them personally? What areas are they still in bondage to and why?

Key Applications: Ask the group to share how they plan to apply what they have learned. They should have prepared for this in the Reflections section of the study, which is at the end of each week's lessons.

See videos & more under resources at abundantlifestudy.com

WEEK 4

Lesson 9 • Abundant Security
The Safety of Grace

Lesson 10 • Abundant Hope
The Certainty of Grace

Lesson 11 • Abundant Plans
The Details of Grace

WEEK 4 OVERVIEW

Prepare: Keep on going! Your diligence in preparation will be a blessing to your group. They need to see The Abundant Life in you! Do the study, look up all the verses, watch the videos, and answer all the questions. Don't forget you too are a student in the study. Ask the Lord to reveal His Word to you as you study. Become very familiar with the major topics, themes, and verses for this week's lessons. Be in prayer all week for you and your group.

Pray: Open the session in prayer. Consider asking one of the participants to pray for the study.

Preview: Watch the video for week 4 as a preview and review. There is only one video this week. It will add seven minutes to the study. Everyone should have watched it at home.

After watching the video together, split into small groups if applicable. The small group leaders should guide the discussion and provide time management to stay on course. Remember you can't cover everything. The goal is to have good discussion and participation in each of the lessons.

Lesson 9 • Abundant Security
The Safety of Grace

EMPHASIZE

Key Points: We are eternally secure in Jesus Christ. A person can't lose their salvation since it involves an irreversible radical change in the nature of their existence and standing before God. Use this foundational truth to get your group overwhelmingly excited and grateful to God that they have eternal life now! It's a present possession that should set us free from the fear of death and from trying to earn or maintain our salvation.

Key Verses: Have your group take turns reading the following verses aloud to the group: John 10:27-30; Romans 8:35-39; Ephesians 1:13-14, 2:8-9; 1 Peter 1:3-5.

ENGAGE

Key Questions: *Why is eternal security so important to The Abundant Life? What are the practical results and benefits of this truth? How can eternal security be liberating?* Also review answers to the questions at the end of the lesson. You will likely need to focus your time on one or two of them that are the most interesting to your group.

Key Insights: Ask the group to share what aspect of Abundant Security is the most profound and amazing to them. What did they learn that they did not know before?

Key Applications: Ask the group to share how they plan to apply what they have learned. They should have prepared for this in the Reflections section of the study, which is at the end of each week's lessons.

See videos & more under resources at abundantlifestudy.com

Lesson 10 • Abundant Hope
The Certainty of Grace

EMPHASIZE

Key Points: As Christians we have biblical hope, a certainty of good things to come which includes heaven, eternal life with God, resurrection, a new glorified body, and all the promises of God, many of which are too incomprehensibly awesome to understand. This should be contrasted with wishful thinking (i.e. I hope I get that job). Get your group excited about real hope because it is liberating and loving.

Key Verses: Have your group take turns reading the following verses aloud to the group: Romans 5:1-5, 15:13; Philippians 3:20-21; 1 John 3:1-3; Hebrews 6:19; 1 Peter 1:3-5.

ENGAGE

Key Question: ***How does biblical hope in the heart empower the Christian life? How should it change our paradigm of life?*** Also review answers to the questions at the end of the lesson. You will likely need to focus your time on one or two of them that are the most interesting to your group.

Key Insights: Ask the group to share which amazing hope from God is most exciting to them. What did they learn about hope that they didn't know before?

Key Applications: Ask the group to share how they plan to apply what they have learned. They should have prepared for this in the Reflections section of the study, which is at the end of each week's lessons.

Lesson 11 • Abundant Plans
The Details of Grace

EMPHASIZE

Key Points: God has an amazing personal plan for our lives that is designed to bring Him glory and to transform us into the image of Jesus Christ. This plan is the reason that we were created, and there is no true meaning or fulfillment in life apart from it. Emphasize how God is intricately personal in our lives if we let Him guide us and speak to us. Get your group on fire to discover His plan now. Encourage them it is never too late to start. This lesson should culminate our preparation for Part II: Abundant Response. If your group is grateful, amazed, excited, and curious, then this will drive them to seek God, praise Him, and surrender to Him so that they can enjoy His plan.

Key Verses: Have your group take turns reading the following verses aloud to the group: Ephesians 2:10; Psalm 139:13-18; Romans 8:28-31; Proverbs 3:5-6.

ENGAGE

Key Question: **Are you walking in and enjoying the plan that the Lord has for your life?** Also review answers to the questions at the end of the lesson. You will likely need to focus your time on one or two of them that are the most interesting to your group.

Key Insights: Ask the group to share which aspect of Abundant Plans is most profound to them. Which is the most intriguing to them personally? What did they learn that was new?

Key Applications: Ask the group to share how they plan to apply what they have learned. They should have prepared for this in the Reflections section of the study, which is at the end of each week's lessons.

See videos & more
under resources at
abundantlifestudy.com

THE
ABUNDANT
LIFE
leader guide

PART II
WEEKS 5-6

PART II
ABUNDANT RESPONSE
Abundant Relationship

→ **THE HEALTHY HEART & HEART EXAMINATION** ←

WEEK 5

Lesson 12 • Abundant Surrender

The Discovery of Relationship

Lesson 13 • Abundant Praise

The Gratitude of Relationship

Lesson 14 • Abundant Words

The Communication of Relationship

WEEK 5 OVERVIEW

Prepare: Keep it up! You have made it to Part II. We are now going to transition into our abundant response to God. If your response is zealous and excited, then your groups will be too. Emphasize to your group that this is the pivotal part in the study where what we have learned causes a response on our part towards God. The fire is kept burning by preparation through studying, praying, watching the videos, answering the questions, and meditating on the Scriptures. Pass this along to your group so they stay ablaze!

Pray: Open the session in prayer. Consider asking one of the participants to pray for the study.

Preview: Watch the video for Part II Overview and Week 5 as a preview and review. There are two videos this week. They will add twelve minutes to the study.

After watching the videos together, split into small groups if applicable. The small group leaders should guide the discussion and provide time management to stay on course. Remember you can't cover everything. The goal is to have good discussion and participation in each of the lessons.

Lesson 12 • Abundant Surrender
The Discovery of Relationship

EMPHASIZE

Key Points: Surrendering to the Lord is not giving up anything of eternal importance. Instead, it is discovering God's eternal plan for our lives. It is a response to God motivated by gratitude, excitement, and a desire to know the One who died for us. It is making God number one! Surrender is a process that matures. No one is ever fully surrendered at all times. You will want to really motivate your group by emphasizing how awesome the Lord is based upon Part I of the study. Brag and boast about what Jesus has done for them so they want to know Him. It's opportunity not obligation. Emphasize at the end of the lesson that, to the same degree that we are not surrendered, our Christian growth and life with the Lord will be hindered.

Key Verses: Have your group take turns reading the following verses aloud to the group: Romans 12:1-2; Psalm 29:2; Philippians 3:7-11; Matthew 16:24-27, 22:37-38.

ENGAGE

Key Questions: **Why is it so important that surrender be motivated from gratitude and a desire to know God rather than obligation and expectation (i.e this is what you are supposed to do or ought to do)? Why is surrender the quintessential step in our response to God?** Also review answers to the questions at the end of the lesson. You will likely need to focus your time on one or two of them that are the most interesting to your group.

Key Insights: Ask the group to share what aspect of surrender is the most exciting to them? Which is the most challenging and why? How does viewing surrender as discovery change things?

Key Applications: Ask the group to share how they plan to apply what they have learned. They should have prepared for this in the Reflections section of the study, which is at the end of each week's lessons..

Lesson 13 • Abundant Praise
The Gratitude of Relationship

EMPHASIZE

Key Points: Praise is an outflow of surrender and worship that is a celebration of who God is, what He is like, and everything He has done for us. Praise is a natural response emanating from a heart that is filled with the love, grace, mercy, and compassion of God. Praise does not always have to be verbal but can also be a silent state of the heart that is thanking God and expressing admiration and gratitude for salvation in Jesus Christ. Emphasize to your group that praise should be bursting out of them at the seams after studying Part I. Make sure they understand that they were created to praise God.

Key Verses: Have your group take turns reading the following verses aloud to the group: Psalm 63:3-5, 96:1-13, 146:1-2, 150:1-6; Revelation 5:8-14.

ENGAGE

Key Question: ***Why do we often fail to praise God even when we know His goodness? What is the solution to apathy? Why is praise so important to our Christian life and spiritual health?*** Also review answers to the questions at the end of the lesson. You will likely need to focus your time on one or two of them that are the most interesting to your group.

Key Insights: Ask the group to share what is their favorite reason to praise God.

Key Applications: Ask the group to share how they plan to apply what they have learned. They should have prepared for this in the Reflections section of the study, which is at the end of each week's lessons.

Lesson 14 • Abundant Words
The Communication of Relationship

EMPHASIZE

Key Points: The Bible is the Word of God. Emphasize that it is the literal words of God to us. It is the main way He has chosen to communicate to us. If we are not reading the Word of God, then we have little to no relationship with God. Emphasize that the Word of God and prayer are two critical ingredients in the Christian life as a source of communication and spiritual growth. No Words = No Relationship.

Key Verses: Have your group take turns reading the following verses aloud to the group: John 8:31-32, 14:21-24, 15:7-8; 2 Timothy 3:16-17; 1 Peter 2:1-3.

ENGAGE

Key Question: *Is it possible to really know someone if your never communicate with them? Why is a lack of prayer often a sign of pride?* Also review answers to the questions at the end of the lesson. You will likely need to focus your time on one or two of them that are the most interesting to your group.

Key Insights: Ask the group to share what aspect of the Word of God is most profound to them. What did they learn that they didn't know before?

Key Applications: Ask the group to share how they plan to apply what they have learned. They should have prepared for this in the Reflections section of the study, which is at the end of each week's lessons.

See videos & more under resources at abundantlifestudy.com

WEEK 6

Lesson 15 • Abundant God

The Interaction of Relationship

Lesson 16 • Abundant Repentance

The Conviction of Relationship

Lesson 17 • Abundant Love for God

The Heart of Relationship

Lesson 18 • Abundant Health

The Wellness of Relationship

WEEK 6 OVERVIEW

Prepare: It is critical to continue to be thoroughly prepared. If you want to see your group respond then you must be ready to lead them and exemplify a vibrant response to God. This only comes through diligent preparation. Do the study, look up all the verses, watch the videos and answer all the questions. Ask the Lord to reveal His Word to you as you study. Become very familiar with the major topics, themes, and verses for this week's lessons. Be in prayer all week for you and your group.

This is the biggest week of the study with 5 lessons if you count the Heart Examination. Most weeks have only two-to-three lessons. You might want to plan on an extra thirty minutes this week if possible.

Pray: Open the session in prayer. Consider asking one of the participants to pray for the study.

Preview: Watch the video for week 6 as a preview and review. There is only one video this week but it is longer. It will add seventeen minutes to the study. Everyone should have watched it at home. The video for Heart Examination is not necessary to view in the group setting.

After watching the video together, split into small groups if applicable. The small group leaders should guide the discussion and provide time management to stay on course. Remember you can't cover everything. The goal is to have good discussion and participation in each of the lessons.

See videos & more under resources at abundantlifestudy.com

Lesson 15 • Abundant God
The Interaction of Relationship

EMPHASIZE

Key Points: When we respond to God, He abundantly responds back. The Lord is waiting for us to respond so He can respond back! Emphasize that God wants a personal relationship with us. Get everyone excited that this relationship is real, interactive, rewarding, exciting and personal.

Key Verses: Have your group take turns reading the following verses aloud to the group: John 14:12-14, 17:3; James 4:7-8; Philippians 4:6-7; Proverbs 16:3.

ENGAGE

Key Questions: *How does God answer prayer? How does the Lord guide us into His will when we are seeking it? How does it practically and experientially happen?* Also review answers to the questions at the end of the lesson. You will likely need to focus your time on one or two of them that are the most interesting to your group.

Key Insights: Ask the group to share some personal testimonies of answered prayers and how Jesus led them to do something that was His will for their lives. Ask people to share how the Lord has strengthened them during difficult times.

Key Applications: Ask the group to share how they plan to apply what they have learned. They should have prepared for this in the Reflections section of the study, which is at the end of each week's lessons.

Lesson 16 • Abundant Repentance
The Conviction of Relationship

EMPHASIZE

Key Points: Repentance is God-centered and focused on restoring our relationship with Him. Emphasize to your group that being "sin sensitive" is healthy and protective, like avoiding germs that can be harmful. Christian growth results in a paradoxical, increased awareness of sin that is healthy and humbling. Make sure they understand that repentance is critical to our spiritual health.

Key Verses: Have your group take turns reading the following verses aloud to the group: Psalm 32; 2 Corinthians 7:10; John 16:7-11; 2 Chronicles 7:14; 1 John 1:8-10.

ENGAGE

Key Question: **What is the difference between repentance, remorse, and regret? Why is repentance so important for our relationship with God? Why is it dangerous to ignore conviction and harden our hearts to it?** Also review answers to the questions at the end of the lesson. You will likely need to focus your time on one or two of them that are the most interesting to your group.

Key Insights: Ask the group to describe what conviction by the Holy Spirit feels like. Encourage them to provide examples where they were under conviction, repented, and then restored to a right relationship God. What was it like? How did it feel at each point in the process?

Key Applications: Ask the group to share how they plan to apply what they have learned. They should have prepared for this in the Reflections section of the study, which is at the end of each week's lessons.

Lesson 17 • Abundant Love For God
The Heart of Relationship

Key Points: We should love God with all our hearts because He loved us even when we were still sinners and unsaved. Emphasize that Jesus gave everything for us on the cross and so we should give Him our whole heart. Make sure they understand that loving God is obeying and fulfilling His Word. This means that we must know the Word of God in order to love God.

Key Verses: Have your group take turns reading the following verses aloud to the group: Matthew 22:35-40; 1 John 4:7-8, 5:3, John 14:21-24; Romans 5:8.

ENGAGE

Key Question: *How does Jesus define loving God? How do we get God's agape love flowing through us and empowering us?* Also review answers to the questions at the end of the lesson. You will likely need to focus your time on one or two of them that are the most interesting to your group.

Key Insights: Ask the group to share how defining love as obedience will change their relationship with God. Have them share what other ways they can show love to God that they need to improve upon.

Key Applications: Ask the group to share how they plan to apply what they have learned. They should have prepared for this in the Reflections section of the study, which is at the end of each week's lessons.

Lesson 18 • Abundant Health
The Wellness of Relationship

EMPHASIZE

Key Points: Spiritual health is a state where abundant revelation results in an abundant relationship with God characterized by surrender, worship, prayer and feeding on the Word of God. Spiritual health is essential to Christian growth and a life that glorifies God. Emphasize that we must diligently maintain and look after our spiritual health just like we do for our physical health.

Key Verses: Have your group take turns reading the following verses aloud to the group: Proverb 3:7-8; 1 Peter 2:1-3; Ephesians 5:18; 1 John 2:15-17; Micah 6:8; John 10:27-30.

ENGAGE

Key Question: **What are the most common problems that negatively affect our spiritual health? How can they be treated and cured?** Also review answers to the questions at the end of the lesson. You will likely need to focus your time on one or two of them that are the most interesting to your group.

Key Insights: Ask the group to share what they learned about spiritual health that they did not know before. Ask them why we are so concerned about our physical health but often neglect our spiritual health?

Key Applications: Ask the group to share how they plan to apply what they have learned. They should have prepared for this in the Reflections section of the study, which is at the end of each week's lessons.

 **HEART EXAMINATION**

If time permits ask the group to share what they learned about their spiritual health from the heart examination. This is on page 141 of the study guide.

What areas are healthy?

What areas need some work?

What is their plan to improve their spiritual health?

See videos & more under resources at abundantlifestudy.com

THE

ABUNDANT

LIFE

leader guide

PART III

WEEKS 7-10

PART III
ABUNDANT RESULTS
Abundant Transformation

WEEK 7

LESSON 19 • ABUNDANT GROWTH: THE NEW MAN MATURES

LESSON 20 • ABUNDANT GODLINESS: THE NEW MAN BLOSSOMS

WEEK 8

LESSON 21 • ABUNDANT STRUGGLE: THE NEW MAN STRUGGLES

LESSON 22 • ABUNDANT SUFFERING: THE NEW MAN SUFFERS

LESSON 23 • ABUNDANT VICTORY: THE NEW MAN SUCCEEDS

Abundant Fruit

WEEK 9

LESSON 24 • ABUNDANT LOVE FOR OTHERS: THE FOCUS OF LOVE

LESSON 25 • ABUNDANT GIVING: THE GIVING OF LOVE

WEEK 10

LESSON 26 • ABUNDANT SERVICE: THE SERVANT OF LOVE

LESSON 27 • ABUNDANT HARVEST: THE GOAL OF LOVE

WEEK 7

Lesson 19 • Abundant Growth
The New Man Matures

Lesson 20 • Abundant Godliness
The New Man Blossoms

WEEK 7 OVERVIEW

Prepare: Part III is the last phase of the study. Results! This is what everyone wants. Keep on preparing and studying. Your preparation will greatly help you and your group. It is critical to continue to be thoroughly prepared. Look up all the verses, watch the videos, and answer all the questions. Ask the Lord to reveal His Word to you as you study. Become very familiar with the major topics, themes, and verses for this week's lessons. Be in prayer all week for you and your group. This week focuses on transformation. Be transformed by the power of God!

Pray: Open the session in prayer. Consider asking one of the participants to pray for the study.

Preview: Watch the video for Part III overview and week 7 as a preview and review. There are two videos this week. They will add eleven minutes to the study. Everyone should have watched them at home.

After watching the videos together, split into small groups if applicable. The small group leaders should guide the discussion and provide time management to stay on course. Remember you can't cover everything. The goal is to have good discussion and participation in each of the lessons.

Lesson 19 • Abundant Growth
The New Man Matures

EMPHASIZE

Key Points: We need to grow spiritually. Spiritual growth requires spiritual food, which is the Word of God. Emphasize to your group the need to read ("eat") the Word of God every day as part of a "balanced diet." Christian growth results in a renewing of our mind, an increasing dependency upon God and a slow transformation to be more like Jesus Christ.

Key Verses: Have your group take turns reading the following verses aloud to the group: 1 Peter 2:2-3; Ephesians 1:15-21; Romans 10:17, 12:1-2; John 8:31-32; Philippians 2:3-11.

ENGAGE

Key Questions: *What happens to your health and strength if you stop eating? How does this relate to our need to be in the Word every day? Why do we almost ALWAYS make sure we have time to eat physically but not spiritually? Why do we need our minds renewed?* Also review answers to the questions at the end of the lesson. You will likely need to focus your time on one or two of them that are the most interesting to your group.

Key Insights: Ask the group to share what aspect of spiritual growth that they need the most. What is the most exciting to them? What is the most daunting and why?

Key Applications: Ask the group to share how they plan to apply what they have learned. They should have prepared for this in the Reflections section of the study, which is at the end of each week's lessons. What steps can be taken to make sure we have better growth?

See videos & more under resources at abundantlifestudy.com

Lesson 20 • Abundant Godliness
The New Man Blossoms

Key Points: A Godly person is fulfilling God's purpose for their life. They know Him in a relationship and are glorifying Him with their life by displaying His character. They are becoming more like Jesus by spending time with Jesus in His presence and Word. Emphasize to your group that Godliness encompasses being in a right relationship with God (Part II) and becoming more like Him as a result (Part III). Make sure they understand we cannot make ourselves Godly. Godliness comes naturally when we are healthy and growing as a work of the Holy Spirit. Let them know they need to focus on their relationship and spiritual growth and God will do the rest. It's also important to emphasize that progress is often slow and involves periods of progress and struggle.

Key Verses: Have your group take turns reading the following verses aloud to the group: Galatians 5:22-23; Romans 8:29-30; 1 Corinthians 6:19-20, 10:31; Psalm 86:12.

ENGAGE

Key Question: ***What are the hallmark signs of Godliness in a believer's life? How do we become more like Christ? What can hinder this transformation process?*** Also review answers to the questions at the end of the lesson. You will likely need to focus your time on one or two of them that are the most interesting to your group.

Key Insights: Ask the group to share their experiences in the transformation process to become more like the Lord. What have been some of their victories, failures, and lessons learned?

Key Applications: Ask the group to share how they plan to apply what they have learned. They should have prepared for this in the Reflections section of the study, which is at the end of each week's lessons.

See videos & more
under resources at
abundantlifestudy.com

WEEK 8

Lesson 21 • Abundant Struggle
The New Man Struggles

Lesson 22 • Abundant Suffering
The New Man Suffers

Lesson 23 • Abundant Victory
The New Man Succeeds

WEEK 8 OVERVIEW

Prepare: Week 8 can be tough because we need to study some unpopular topics like suffering. Our nature is to study the things that we know and like and avoid those that we do not. Prepare for this week by asking the Lord to give you a really positive attitude and even be excited about teaching on suffering and struggle. The last topic is our victory anyway! Your diligent preparation will help secure their victory.

Pray: Open the session in prayer. Consider asking one of the participants to pray for the study.

Preview: Watch the video for week 8 as a preview and review. There is only one video this week. It will add twelve minutes to the study.

After watching the video together, split into small groups if applicable. The small group leaders should guide the discussion and provide time management to stay on course. Remember you can't cover everything. The goal is to have good discussion and participation in each of the lessons.

Lesson 21 • Abundant Struggle
The New Man Struggles

Key Points: The Christian life is a war against our flesh/sinful nature, the devil and the world. Emphasize that struggling against these three enemies is not a sign of weakness but of salvation and Christian growth. Victory and conquest require many battles. We, like Joshua in the Old Testament, must engage the enemy, idols, and things that do not belong in the "land" of our hearts in order to drive them out, but this requires war.

Key Verses: Have your group take turns reading the following verses aloud to the group: Galatians 5:16-21; 1 Peter 5:8; 1 John 2:15-17; John 16:33; Joshua 1:1-9.

Key Questions: ***Why do you think God decided to let the flesh/sinful nature remain? What are the implications of our biggest enemy being ourselves?!*** Also review answers to the questions at the end of the lesson. You will likely need to focus your time on one or two of them that are the most interesting to your group.

Key Insights: Ask the group to share how they have battled against the flesh/sinful nature, the world and the devil. How have they had victories and defeats? What did they learn?

Key Applications: Ask the group to share how they plan to apply what they have learned. They should have prepared for this in the Reflections section of the study, which is at the end of each week's lessons.

See videos & more under resources at abundantlifestudy.com

Lesson 22 • Abundant Suffering
The New Man Suffers

EMPHASIZE

Key Points: We live and exist in the middle of a spiritual war in a fallen world ravaged by sin and the enemy. Emphasize we all need to realign how we see both our lives and our existence in relation to this world with biblical reality. Suffering and trials should not only be expected but viewed as opportunities to grow and become more like Jesus. This is radical thinking but it is biblical thinking and the truth that will set us free.

Key Verses: Have your group take turns reading the following verses aloud to the group: 2 Corinthians 1:5; Romans 5:1-5, 8:17-25; 2 Timothy 3:10-12; James 1:2-8.

ENGAGE

Key Questions: *How can trials and suffering be good for us and help us grow spiritually?* Also review answers to the questions at the end of the lesson. You will likely need to focus your time on one or two of them that are the most interesting to your group.

Key Insights: Ask the group to share some personal testimonies of how God used suffering or a trial to grow them spiritually.

Key Applications: Ask the group to share how they plan to apply what they have learned. They should have prepared for this in the Reflections section of the study, which is at the end of each week's lessons.

Lesson 23 • Abundant Victory
The New Man Succeeds

EMPHASIZE

Key Points: All of our power for victory comes from God. God has given us the ability to have victory, but He leaves it up to us to tap into this power by choosing to grow, mature and depend upon Him. We must grow, mature, and be renewed by the power of the Holy Spirit as we submit to God and feed on His Word. Make sure the group understands that victory assumes many battles will be fought. There is no victory if there is no war.

Key Verses: Have your group take turns reading the following verses aloud to the group: Romans 6:1-14, 8:35-37; Galatians 5:22-26; 1 John 5:4-5; Ephesians 4:17-32, 6:10-20.

ENGAGE

Key Questions: *How do we overcome the flesh/sinful nature, the world, and the devil? How do Parts I and II of this study relate to victory?* Also review answers to the questions at the end of the lesson. You will likely need to focus your time on one or two of them that are the most interesting to your group.

Key Insights: Ask the group to share how God has given them the victory over sin, the flesh/sinful nature, the enemy and the world. Have them share a few short personal testimonies.

Key Applications: Ask the group to share how they plan to apply what they have learned. They should have prepared for this in the Reflections section of the study, which is at the end of each week's lessons.

WEEK 9

Lesson 24 • Abundant Love for Others

The Focus of Love

Lesson 25 • Abundant Giving

The Giving of Love

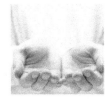

WEEK 9 OVERVIEW

Prepare: This week we begin to study the fruit of being a healthy and growing Christian in a healthy relationship with the Lord. Continue to pray and to be fully prepared to lead your group. Dig deep into these Scriptures to discover what God has to teach you in His Word. Let your group see how exciting these results are!

Pray: Open the session in prayer. Consider asking one of the participants to pray for the study.

Preview: Watch the video for week 9 as a preview and review. There is only one video this week. It will add eight minutes to the study. Everyone should have watched it at home.

After watching the video together, split into small groups if applicable. The small group leaders should guide the discussion and provide time management to stay on course. Remember you can't cover everything. The goal is to have good discussion and participation in each of the lessons.

Lesson 24 • Abundant Love for Others
The Focus of Love

EMPHASIZE

Key Points: The heart of love is unselfish giving of ourselves, and the focus of love is others. God is the source of the love that we need. God is love and we need His love to flow through us into other people's lives. This makes us dependent upon Jesus. Emphasize to your group that this requires that they must first be right with the Lord personally before they can truly be right with others.

Key Verses: Have your group take turns reading the following verses aloud to the group: John 15:12-17; Matthew 22:34-40; Philippians 2:4; Galatians 5:13; 1 Thessalonians 5:25.

ENGAGE

Key Questions: *How can we unselfishly love, serve, and look out for others when we are so selfish to the core and live in a society that is self-centered?* Also review answers to the questions at the end of the lesson. You will likely need to focus your time on one or two of them that are the most interesting to your group.

Key Insights: Ask the group to share how they are able to love others as Jesus commands.

Key Applications: Ask the group to share how they plan to apply what they have learned. They should have prepared for this in the Reflections section of the study, which is at the end of each week's lessons.

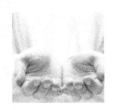

Lesson 25 • Abundant Giving
The Giving of Love

Key Points: Everything belongs to God. This includes our money, our possessions, and even our own existence. Emphasize to your group that seeing everything (including ourselves) as belonging to God provides the right paradigm to be a giver. Also, it is critical to understand that we need to first give ourselves to God to be able to properly give anything else. Giving makes us more like God, draws us closer to God, enables others to see God, and helps us let go of materialism and our fixation on ourselves.

Key Verses: Have your group take turns reading the following verses aloud to the group: Matthew 16:24-27; 2 Corinthians 8:1-15; Proverbs 3:9-10; 1 John 3:16-19.

ENGAGE

Key Questions: ***How does giving ourselves to God and others make us like Christ? How is giving an aspect of God's love?*** Also review answers to the questions at the end of the lesson. You will likely need to focus your time on one or two of them that are the most interesting to your group.

Key Insights: Ask the group to share where they struggle the most in giving? Is it personal surrender, giving to others, or financial? Why do they think this is the case?

Key Applications: Ask the group to share how they plan to apply what they have learned. They should have prepared for this in the Reflections section of the study, which is at the end of each week's lessons.

WEEK 10

Lesson 26 • Abundant Service
The Servant of Love

Lesson 27 • Abundant Harvest
The Goal of Love

WEEK 10 OVERVIEW

Prepare: This is the final week! You are almost there. Finish strong by delving deep into God's Word this week. Pray for your group and let the Lord show you about Christian service and His heart for the lost. Make sure to remind your group that this is just the start of The Abundant Life. It's a process that never ends until we go home to be with the Lord. We must keep reading His Word and fueling the fire to serve and know Him so we can become more like Him.

Pray: Open the session in prayer. Consider asking one of the participants to pray for the study.

Preview: Watch the video for week 10 as a preview and review. There are two videos this week (Week 10 and Conclusion). They will add ten minutes to the study.

After watching the videos together, split into small groups if applicable. The small group leaders should guide the discussion and provide time management to stay on course. Remember you can't cover everything. The goal is to have good discussion and participation in each of the lessons.

Lesson 26 • Abundant Service

The Servant of Love

EMPHASIZE

Key Points: The Lord Jesus Christ is the perfect servant. We are most like the Lord when we are serving Him and others. Emphasize to your group that God has a special place and way for them to serve Him. Encourage them to serve from gratitude and love rather than obligation and expectation. Remember we serve from the cross not as a way to get to the cross. We serve and love God because of what He has already done; not as a way to earn His favor. Finally, the power and the ability to serve come from God Himself. This is another reason we need to constantly seek Him.

Key Verses: Have your group take turns reading the following verses aloud to the group: Mark 9:33-35, 10:34-35; 2 Timothy 2:3-4; 1 Corinthians 9:19-23; Philippians 2:1-11.

ENGAGE

Key Questions: **How is it possible for someone to be busy serving others without serving God? How can we avoid this error?** Also review answers to the questions at the end of the lesson. You will likely need to focus your time on one or two of them that are the most interesting to your group.

Key Insights: Ask the group to share how they are serving God and others. Has anyone ever been busy serving other people but ignoring the Lord at the same time?

Key Applications: Ask the group to share how they plan to apply what they have learned. They should have prepared for this in the Reflections section of the study, which is at the end of each week's lessons.

See videos & more under resources at abundantlifestudy.com

Lesson 27 • Abundant Harvest
The Goal of Love

EMPHASIZE

Key Points: At the end of the day behind everything going on, God is all about saving people. If people are not being saved and brought into the kingdom in a relationship with God, then Jesus died in vain. Emphasize to your group that we are only responsible for sharing the Gospel in a loving and appropriate way. The results are up to God and the person hearing, not us.

Key Verses: Have your group take turns reading the following verses aloud to the group: Matthew 9:37-38, 28:18-20; 2 Corinthians 5:18-21; 2 Timothy 1:8-12; 1 Peter 3:15-16.

ENGAGE

Key Questions: **_Why are we sometimes ashamed of sharing the Gospel? What is the cure for this?_** Also review answers to the questions at the end of the lesson. You will likely need to focus your time on one or two of them that are the most interesting to your group.

Key Insights: Ask the group to share some personal testimonies of how God has used them to share the Gospel. What mistakes have they made and what have they learned from them? Have someone describe a time when they knew God was nudging them to share and they did not. Why didn't they? What can we learn from this?

Key Applications: Ask the group to share how they plan to apply what they have learned. They should have prepared for this in the Reflections section of the study, which is at the end of each week's lessons.

OTHER WORKS

OTHER RESOURCES BY DR. GREG VIEHMAN

THE GOD DIAGNOSIS

A SUCCESSFUL PHYSICIAN MAKES THE MOST STARTLING AND UNEXPECTED DIAGNOSIS OF HIS LIFE.

Unsettled by the mysteries of purpose and destiny, Dr. Viehman takes the reader on an emotionally palpable and transforming journey through cynicism, skepticism and discovery. The God Diagnosis is a detailed and compelling testimony of a skilled surgeon who himself undergoes a "heart transplant."

www.goddiagnosis.com

You can purchase 'The God Diagnosis' at these digital locations:

Also available in multiple languages.

EVERLAS†ING STRENGTH

www.everlastingstrength.org

Everlasting Strength seeks to demonstrate the love of Jesus Christ by evangelism, biblical teaching, and charitable giving so that people may know God in a growing, personal, and saving relationship that increasingly glorifies Him with their lives. Visit Everlasting Strength to sign up for Dr. Viehman's blog, view his testimony and select speaking engagements, and interact with other biblical resources to grow in the Lord and be on fire for the Gospel! The Lord and His Word are awesome and something to be excited about!

www.everlastingstrength.org

CPSIA information can be obtained
at www.ICGtesting.com
Printed in the USA
BVOW05s1004230717
489693BV00012B/81/P